the abyss is staring back

D1598425

the abyss is staring back

a hybrid poetry collection

nat raum

QUERENCIA PRESS

© Copyright 2023
nat raum

ISBN 978 1 959118 24 4

www.querenciapress.com

First Published in 2023

Querencia Press, LLC
Chicago IL

Printed & Bound in the United States of America

also by nat raum

self portrait as several clusters of stars

the fine line

specter dust

you stupid slut

preparatory school for the end of the world

contents

stasis (i).. 11

    i have a lot of questions 13

    episodic memory 14

    personal evolution as alchemy 15

    a haibun of indifference to my body 16

    rot around the edges 17

    daisy.. 18

    assigned cybernetic at birth 19

    who has a gps map of hell i can borrow? 21

    free & for sale (iso wholeness).. 22

    failed self portrait as link from the legend of zelda: breath of the wild
.... 23

    you are missing from me... 24

    my personal sunk cost fallacy.. 25

    wholesome crying.. 26

    voidspeak (skinned) 28

    i hate so much about the things that you choose to be 29

    in which i kind of want to live in schitt's creek 30

    clamshell 32

flux 34

    in which i write myself backwards 36

    are you afraid of the intimacy?.. 37

    in which i download hinge for the first time 38

    free & for sale (selling shame) 40

    please don't super like me; i don't want that kind of pressure 41

    soliloquy.. 42

    thank you for never texting me again 44

    hinge profile rejects... 45

my personal etymology 47

and i'm honestly feeling so attacked right now 48

chicken 49

hindsight is 20/20 and also 2020 50

the fine line between self-loving and self-loathing 51

voidspeak (sheltered)..52

this user is thinking about death 53

stasis (ii) 55

you may find yourself...57

my personal trauma watershed....................................58

searching..59

in which dread pools and begins to percolate 61

eroding 62

the root of traction is to drag 63

we have been trying to reach you about your body's extended warranty 64

in which i perforate 65

save changes to untitled? 68

free & for sale (yard sard) 69

consequences 70

self-assessment essay rejects.....................................71

a thicket of weeds..73

the duality of void 74

scorpius 75

hot sugar crush...76

i heart my fat ass 77

self portrait as a food blogger.....................................78

acknowledgements...81

stasis (i)

i have a lot of questions

what do you do when the abyss stares back? what do you do when you no longer have a joker origin story, but a joker origin trilogy? why are my feet so firmly planted on broken earth?

why was i bred during the years where the world kept inventing more ways to break your heart? what would baby blonde me in a polyester plaid jumper say if i told her my first love and i used to fight in public online? that i'd never have met my college partner if not for an anonymous question on my blog? that i've lived with someone who started out a stranger on the internet?

does the moon change phases in the night sometimes? is it possible that the waxing crescent i saw when the sun first went down has swelled up before my eyes so minutely that i've just noticed it now? whether or not this can happen to the moon, can it happen to other things, like people you used to love?

when you take a picture of the moon on your phone, you know how you can never capture the craters or glow the way they actually look? do you know that everyone i've let love me has shied even further away from my camera than the moon? do you think that's why no one has ever believed i could choose wisely, because i didn't have anything to show for it? is it stupid to compare a lover to the moon, knowing he'll never be as graceful, as silent, or as steady? is it worth letting anyone see my collection of pixelated photos of a shadow blurred with moonlight?

will the internet be what breaks the earth, in the end? can the internet break your heart, too?

episodic memory
— after "assumptions" by richard hugo

i.   i am the most loathsome weight
to shoulder. i am the calamity responsible
for ruins, a catastrophe by comparison
to how i've broken down, how termites hollow-
out wooden foundations behind sheetrock
and subfloor (only discovered once misplaced
steps pull me through the kitchen floor).
i was made like this. it is prophecy.

ii.   god said *fuck nat raum, in particular.*
i am bound in my mother's arms in a private
waiting room, eyes boring into ceiling tiles
as the lord abides the crack in my grandfather's
voice telling us to call saint mary's church. i couldn't
hope to forget every floor's fluorescent lights, flickering
like trick candles for a vigil, nor every snag in carpet and
crack in linoleum that trips me on my way to the elevator.

iii.   each night i will close my eyes
and float in this chasm within myself
until i wake. if not, i come to
after visions of car crashes, shipwrecks,
pulling away from embraces to find lovers
past superseding lovers present. eventually
there will be twenty-four or even twelve or six
or two hours i remember every minute of. until then
stasis covers my eyes and whispers:
guess what? still here.

personal evolution as alchemy

gather: kindling,
waste ingot of spite.

inside skin,
make heat.
make light.

melt copper
like dessert mints
on greedy tongues.

mold to desired
shape.

a haibun of indifference to my body

there is a home in this body, only in that i am here and i always have been, the same way i have always been able to drift northwest to a brown wooden house in green valley north. and maybe that's not all she has in common with the house, as they are both falling apart. i don't remember the last time there wasn't a pinch or spasm up my spine or a day where my knuckles weren't at least half swollen by dinnertime. but unlike the valley house, my body doesn't greet me like i belong at her threshold, marveling at the ways earth really does always smell like dirt and rain this far outside the city, let alone inside your waterlogged and woodpeckered walls.

and yet, there is probably still a home in this body for that reason, because i only ever set myself on that northwest drift in the first place because real home is the limestone rowhouse that had once felt like stability, is as eager to drive me out as this body seems to be. i'd sooner jump from my skin, given the choice, but that doesn't mean there isn't a part of me that can still find a speck of solace in *knowing* her—her tethers that feel like a hogtie most of the time, yet still cradle me when there are no woodpeckered walls, no verdant valley that smells like soil or lava-lamp oasis behind a locked door. but to know can be to love or to hate, and i can't find that same size speck of love in myself whenever i walk into a room, and i am only her, only body, only woman, not me.

is home not just some
place you're used to, at the end
of the day? discuss.

rot around the edges

today i heard the corpus christi churchbells
in the county, christ's very own
bodybells chiming a solstice christmas
in my head. what i felt was kind of like

the way i cry whenever i read something
too pure on twitter because i just want my own
chance to be wholesome. the phantom chimes
are here to remind me i'm still corporeal

on this marble where the internet does not care
what you hold dear. it will break you if you let it
(just like he did). i only have feelings anymore
when i'm reattached to this body through some

sort of quiet anguish, like flaking skin from my
lips, with flattened cuspids.

daisy

elegant and sparkling
bursts of pearblossom
strawberry rosebud
prickle like a parallel
timeline where fashion
meant style and self,

when my teen novel
heroines didn't give
a damn and when
i didn't either, until
after over a decade,
it dawned: i gave
everything.

assigned cybernetic at birth

when you suddenly needed a training bra
at nine years old, the parents all bought you
and your friends the same friendly illustrated book
predicting the future of your body. you didn't know

yet how much you could covet changes to your flesh
home—there was no chapter on what happens
when splenetic nerves and the heft of your chest
invade you until your skin now houses a hovel.

you didn't have words for the wondering what
else your body could be. you spent your lazy dial-up
summers reading the same two britannica entries,
boyish curiosity about differences in anatomy

eating you alive (shame arriving later to clear
your cache). you pretended you were looking for a photo
of a frost-blue neon lucite bed you forgot to screengrab
for your dream bedroom powerpoint mood board,

not the man without clothes google images showed
right next to the bed on page 30something. you didn't talk
about your exponential wondering as you aged—about
your body or your best friends' lips. (there wasn't enough

space in your head for that sort of thing back then.)
you thought you knew what longing felt like, smoothing
your curls with a heat iron and chasing boy after boy
who'd sold you on the idea of him, somehow.

you couldn't have known it actually feels like your body,
seventeen years later: sickness when you're standing too long,
spandex subtracting the skin under your t-shirt pocket, and
another wondering about what else you could have known.

who has a gps map of hell i can borrow?

i drive spindlefingered > through twilight > in no hurry > there's
no night sky where we're headed > there are only two types of
acquaintances > people i root for > people i don't > people who
went to festivals in high school to see bands i still haven't heard
of > who didn't wear rainboots even though the sky always
opened up > onto the lawn at merriweather post pavilion > who
slid downhill in muck and cutoff denim shorts > envy drives me
> not jealousy > that someone is kissing my boyfriend > that
anyone is kissing at all > while i > leon s. kennedy > dash
through a plague-ridden village with a wiimote > seek the heat of
regenerator masses through the scope of a rifle > tell my spanish
teacher i practiced spanish over break > *cogélo* means *go get him* >
morir es vivir > *to die is to live* > and i'll be there soon i swear

free & for sale (iso wholeness)

hi everybody, i am looking for the things
i think are missing inside me because
that's what everyone else cited as my fatal
flaw: not enough. of what? i don't really know
what i'm looking for, but i'm open to learning,
from everyone and anyone who looks my way,
exactly what is wrong with me. hit me
up if you can help with something like this
and we'll make it work.

failed self portrait as link from the legend of zelda: breath of the wild

the soundscape of a baltimore summer
is just the hum of a fan that never works
well enough and can never be blotted
out by any amount of dulcet woodwinds
or tarrey town rain. i wonder, though,

do you think late life transness is sort of
like when someone says to link you're
actually hylian and the chimes ascend
in celebration because it suddenly makes
sense? and i'm really just asking this
because i kind of felt like that when i read
cis people don't genderswap

in their daydreams and i want to know
if my prophecy is coming before i become
entombed in the plaster of an efficiency apartment.

you are missing from me

in french, you don't say "i miss you."
you say "tu me manques"
which means "you are missing from me,"
and i think that's beautiful.

in french, you don't say "i have died."
you say "je suis mort"
which means "i am death,"
and i think that's beautiful.

in french, you don't call it "your body."
you call it "ton mère nourricière qui t'enterre"[1]
which means "your nourishing mother who buries you,"
and i think that's beautiful.

in french, i can't call you "the love of my life."
i say "la douleur exquise"
which means "exquisite pain,"
and i think that's beautiful.

---

[1] inspired by « La terre » by Elisabeth Anais, *Le Petit Prince (Extraits du Spectacle Musical)*, Mercury 2022

my personal sunk cost fallacy

lately i wonder if why i can't quit the people i could never have hoped to please is because i can see past lives when i close my eyes. have i known my enemies in other centuries? do i shout forward at myself to keep going since i hold them dear somewhere else? i'm still a child, you know, despite the chill the last score has sent vibrating through my veins, nightmares of past paramours in chainmail and lace and loincloths. i could stroke velvet in my dreams and still not see truth through the evergreens of arbitrary tenacity.

wholesome crying

1.

the shriners children's hospital commercial
a picture book about a young penguin with anxiety learning
breath work

santa riding on a fire truck through my parents' neighborhood
a gif my classmate sent of a bunny helping another into a boat,
saying *welcome aboard*

2.

the frozen edamame packaging that said *this little green gem
nourishes your heart and soul*
the band-aid box that told me i would be just fine
talking trains named chuggington in the amtrak train travel safety
video

3.

two fuzzy s'mores on the front of my mom's mother's day card
(they said *i love you* and *i love you s'more* to each other)
a sign outside the florist that said *you are as welcome as the flowers in may*

voidspeak (skinned)

skinned asks: how long can you scrape by before your entire body is covered in flesh wounds?

the void says: skinned, you can't want like you do and not fall down most of the time. you wear catastrophe like threadbare blue jeans, the kind you'd call a second set of legs after enough spin cycles have worn them down. you don't feel their incremental lightening each time you pull their soft limbholes out of the dryer while they're still warm and the machine is still clicking—you only notice once your fingers thread through the holes and you ball the pants up in the corner behind the door. instead of running from them, weave yourself into the tears you discover in the cotton's seams. wade your toes into the shadows that loom so tall and deep from the baseboard each night that they could well house whatever you believe waits for you in the dark. but remember, in the end, even once the frights subside, the only thing that awaits you is yourself.

i hate so much about the things that you choose to be

sometimes when i sink far enough

into my own silt, i imagine myself
swamped elsewhere; i see my waist-fat
cinched in, suburban kitchen

tile underfoot and a man with a matching
ring next to me who once said it was
mildly disturbing i tracked

my body count. i imagine my imagination
recalling what i pictured my Xbox saying about it.
achievement unlocked: emotional

wreckage! finally learn what it means to feel.

in which i kind of want to live in schitt's creek

mostly i am just thinking
about what it would be like to lose
my entire life and move to a town
in the middle of nowhere and
live in a motel with my parents.

of course i'm thinking about
my people because no one i know
would dare miss my wedding
like david's new york friends
and i'm thinking about a life without
pan-fried meat dumplings delivered
to my door or the clop and jangle
of a passing arabber outside

but i'm also thinking about learning
to sleep to the sound of locusts
and ordering soup and sandwich
lunches off a vinyl menu. i'm thinking
about horribly-named roadside dive bars
and only enough clothes for a motel
wardrobe and the kind of quirks i'd roll
my eyes at back in the city but i think
i could learn to smile at

somewhere else. mostly i am
just thinking about how i might be
terrified to start over but how much
i would still leap for an excuse
to know literally anything else.

clamshell

i pluck a clamshell off
the beach in stardew valley.
the popup tells me,

someone lived here once

and suddenly i envy all
creatures with shells for skin,
how their outsides exist

so separately from their actual
beings and how easily

they move along
after outgrowing it.

flux

in which i write myself backwards

i am crying out to myself on the night of february 6, 2011.

i am erasing every letter i handwrote to my future self to open on my birthday a year later while staring directly back at where i'd come from. i am redacting every single wonderful thing i ever wrote about my first love in hopes it will bleach away that part of the past. i am hoping i can rewrite it queerer.

i am wondering why i felt he was so worthy of every beautiful word i had that i gave him all of them and ran out for years. i am begging myself to stop saving so many pieces of me for him. i am resenting all of the new kinds of self-flagellation he filled my hollow spaces with. i am mourning how long i tried to take the shape he wanted me to fill.

i am dreaming of a state fair and festival summer, sugarfloss sunsets, and philosophy-lipgloss-kisses where my pretty friends all taste like red velvet birthday cakes. i am living the life i reblogged on tumblr. i am hovering over youth on a high dive like it's my first time staring downward and wondering if i should. i am slowing through the surface of a pane of glass until my whole body knows the wonder of being hugged on every side by water.

i am thinking of how now, i know queerness is like water in that way. i am asking why i ever let someone stand in the way of autonomy. i am wishing i could have felt as proud, just once, by the time i wrote that letter—february 6, 2011.

are you afraid of the intimacy?

co-star today: "you can move on to the next chapter, even if the one you're living in doesn't feel finished."

it's funny how the loneliness doesn't set in until i'm in a room full of people asking me what happened, why we broke up, if i'm dating someone new, and why not? (god, i wish i hadn't brought my ex on my family vacation last year.) i watch the freckles on my arms multiply, just like his did last summer when he was here with me. the list of things i don't want in my next partner keeps growing. i'm so tired of mediocre clit rubbing from men who won't even let me choose the music.

in which i download hinge for the first time

we'll get along if
you're a christian, love sports, and are constantly joyful

believe it or not, i
have been hit in the face with a bowling ball

i'm actually legitimately bad at
dating apps

biggest risk i've taken
gas station sushi

i'm convinced that
avril lavigne is dead, and somewhere in the mountains of canada
is a cloning facility churning out fake avrils to throw us off the
trail

we'll get along if
u keep it 💯 at all times

i'm convinced that
seth macfarlane is the best artist of our generation

you should leave a comment if
you have low standards

never have i ever
been to IKEA

i'm a regular at
bass pro shop

my most irrational fear
humpback whales

if loving this is wrong, i don't want to be right
kanye west

free & for sale (selling shame)

i am selling the shroud that falls
upon me when i should be embarrassed—

it served me well, but i don't think i need it
anymore. great used condition; well-loved,

but a lot of life left. taking up space on the
shelf next to a secret agent barbie cd-rom

pickup only, please? my body isn't broken down
just yet, but i'm planning for the day when

i creak like a floorboard and screech like a muffler
skimming the speed bumps on my street.

please don't super like me;
i don't want that kind of pressure

there's something comforting about going back on dating apps after a long absence and seeing all of the people you left behind who are still on dating apps. it would of course be better if they didn't feel the need to notice your reappearance and ask how you've been (well, you see, some days i only passively want to die instead of actively wanting to die) and why you're back (the person i thought i was going to marry ripped my heart into a thousand tiny pieces).

soliloquy

1.

i just got emotional about something stupid again.
i hate being soft.

sometimes i think my life would be easier if i'd ever gotten the
chance to be pure.
tragedy is such a constant, i don't know what "childlike" means.

god, i just want to be wholesome for a day.

2.

i don't want to talk to anyone,
but i spend too much time inside my head.

i need a shower
(i need a life).

3.

i would literally die to stop being sad like this.

(*oh.*)

4.

i feel like it looks like i'm holding it together well?
does it look like i'm holding it together well?

do i give a fuck if it doesn't?

thank you for never texting me again

the problem with realizing that absolutely none of your relationships ever have been healthy is that when a new prospect is actually proceeding normally, you have absolutely no idea how to respond and are vaguely annoyed at everything, from how wholesome and surface-level everything feels, to how you haven't sent a single photo of your boobs yet.

if *the real housewives of new york city* has taught me one thing, it's that there is something that *destroys* grown women about thinking this is the rest of your life and being proven horribly wrong, so basically i feel better. there is something oddly comforting about the escapism present in the act of watching reality tv. you may have just eaten an entire 8 ounce burrata by yourself in one sitting, but at least you didn't take off your prosthetic leg and slam it down on top of a table during a dinner party. on television.

hinge profile rejects

i go crazy for
~~getting really high and staying up past midnight talking to~~
~~strangers on discord~~
~~men who do the bare minimum~~
researching hurricanes on wikipedia

i'll introduce you to my family if
~~i know you won't make a fool of both yourself and me~~
i know my mom will be nice to you

an overshare
~~i thought i might be engaged by now~~
~~i drink roughly three dr. peppers a day~~
~~i'm pretty sure i'm getting ghosted again~~
~~i'm high as fuck whenever i'm on this app~~
~~sometimes i listen to fall out boy for a day and a half straight~~
~~i'm real fucking depressed~~
~~there are so many, how could i pick just one?~~
pass

my most controversial opinion is
~~liking or not liking something popular isn't a stand-in for a~~
~~personality~~
~~most of you are really boring~~
private school should be illegal

my love language is
~~receiving validation~~
receiving gifts

i'll know it's time to delete hinge when
~~someone finally realizes i'm a fucking catch~~
~~i feel 100% comfortable with someone~~
i don't feel like i'm performing for you

my personal etymology

i've forgotten languages again. is *muñeca* doll or wrist or both? how do you say *oven* in french again? why is the only latin verb i remember *expugno/are/avi/atum*; to capture by force, as i once tabbed in my textbook? why don't i remember things i recited in my sleep? who took my non-english words? was it the way boys wormed into my brain-matter through the stem? the way my cerebellum short-circuited first before allowing company inside? was i ever fluent in anything if i have to use google translate now? did i lose spanish slang to a lover? will i eventually lose the vignettes i have in english to my mind?

and i'm honestly feeling so attacked right now

since the inception of my very first pop
punk fan blog, i've used the internet
like i have nothing to hide. online,
i could be the kind of beauty

my relatives regaled— some soft grunge
darling or wanderlust's golden rays, so
camera-happy there are image-based

primary sources to prove i invented dark
academia in 2011. a prep school's wallflower,

i could thrive where everything was beautiful

and i knew it wouldn't hurt later.[2]

---

[2] the last two lines reference Kurt Vonnegut's *Slaughterhouse-Five*
(Random House, 1969).

chicken

an herb-crusted chicken
breast's vein on my plate
tickles the fear in me,
and again i ask

if the dizziness really
just comes from how i hate
the way veins spiderweb

blood through skin or if
i hate them because

terror courses through them too.

hindsight is 20/20 and also 2020

there was a scene in *vanderpump rules* where kristen is yelling at
sandoval about how she "wanted to marry him and now she has
to consider something else" and before i'd been in the marriage
arena, i cackled when i heard it. now that i've lost that for myself,
i almost feel like i should go find her and apologize. i see myself
on tv a lot. i was watching 90 day fiance with him not long before
we broke up, and this girl on tv told her man who had moved
halfway across the world for her that he wasn't her soul mate
(someone else was). and it's not like i would have ever admitted it
out loud, but it was kind of a mood?

i just felt like my soul mate would love me for more than my
image in a mirror.

the fine line between self-loving and self-loathing[3]

you don't have to prove yourself to anyone.

(i'm doing shitty too so i really feel this.)

experiment with tenderness.

(i just like....want to know when this is gonna stop. not just the missing him but the uncertainty of existing in this world.)

almost touch.

(unfortunately, the missing is still a big part of it. i crave stability.)

where do these strange ideas come from?

(this. all of this.)

---

[3] this cento is written from Co-Star daily app notifications and excerpts from a group text conversation from July 2020.

voidspeak (sheltered)

sheltered asks: how do you know when it's safe to leave the place you've been hiding?

the void says: oh, sheltered, do you remember when you were seventeen or so, and you waited out an afternoon thunderstorm in a boathouse? think of how safe you really were. remember when you were even younger, and a bolt of lightning split the lake water ten feet from your face and twenty from where you stood under that roof? thank god your view of relativity was simpler back then.

listen, it's clear you're not so attached to whatever barrier you've found to separate you and your nightmares, so i'll bite: shingleshacks might protect you from the next squall, but they won't withstand the whole chain of storms.

this user is thinking about death

you know that thing i said earlier about passively wanting to die?

i'm starting to realize that it's easy to passively wish you are dead when you have spent roughly a year and a half of your life being consumed by the notion that you existed to please someone else. i am an accessory as useless as a fascinator or a fake pocket.

remember that you've done this before.
remember that you can:
- crack your own back
- dry your own tears
- exist before someone
- exist after someone
- go on

stasis (ii)

you may find yourself

i'm high and tired, and the list of things i care about is dwindling by the minute. i will wake up tomorrow sore-hipped, wristbones wailing for giving in, but this sort of restless demands i abandon my prescribed posture-pose and corkscrew my limbs until my body is a shorehouse to be swallowed by the sea. sometimes i will wake between now and then (sometimes more than one time) and my throat will lurch through the kind of cough where you spit mucus like slugs, chip itself dry until i reach for a flat nightstand seltzer. when the last of my pieces have finally drifted again, my synapses will remember that i absolutely cannot help myself from being crushed by the sorrow of stasis. i will turn over and instead of blinking away hours when the black of my vision splits into dots, i will face the flood that carried me here, no matter how high i've built my stilts or how many floors i've climbed. i will tread in riptides and remember i am not actually standing as still as i think i am. i'm just in the same place as always.

my personal trauma watershed

i wrote you and i like an epitaph. you can't have our kind of self awareness without knowing how likely it is we will fall, apart or together. sometimes (most times) it's the knowing that gets to me. it's the clear path i can trace with a shaking pointer finger back to where it began, stopping where all of the tributaries converge to explain how they got there and what new trouble they brought when the streams finally eroded their way together as one. it's the way i can see you do this on your own without the language for it and the way i want to help but i'm terrified of falling into the trap of fixer again.

searching

1.

why do all of my joints hurt a lot
can carpal tunnel mimic arthritis symptoms

body hurts for no reason
stabbing pain below shoulder blades
stabbing pain entire body

how much is too much caffeine for a disabled 25 year old afab
with anxiety

2.

body swells at night
good lighters for arthritis
full body compression sleeve

is my body mad at me
is my headache and fatigue being caused by the omicron variant
or tension and depression
can extended dissociation make regaining consciousness harder
nerve pain and migraine headaches

3.

will it ever stop hurting to think about times in my life i was ten
times as alive as i am now
how much of a major cardiac event does medicaid cover

heart attack age 26
fastest way to die of natural causes

is my stomach swallowing itself

in which dread pools and begins to percolate

i am gripped each time i am running late
by thoughts which pile up, then incubate.
with obligations countless
and hours sold, near thankless,
i resent living in a fascist state.

eroding

bruiseblue, i fold my hands and my
knuckles throb in sync into each other's,
sinew, the guts behind a tumbled shell
still not so malleable as they are
forgettable; not so kneaded by

my barest nightmares anymore as
sparring with the ghosts of their grip.
how much of living is sifting ashes
through the sieve of moth-shredded
organza curtain between me

and the clarity i seek? which way
do i travel to leave behind my body
and all it's seen and heard? and
how many holes in shell or silk
is enough to see through?

the root of traction is to drag

i resent that the only way out is through. i resent that i can't pull out latin roots anymore without thinking about you and how i never told you i used to keep a list of them in the back of my middle school science notebook. before i grew too tired, i started saving things in a folder when they reminded me of you. the more times i write the word "traction" over and over again into a spreadsheet talking about a brand message, the less energy i have to be sad every single time i remember that the root of traction is to drag and that the root of all suffering is attachment.

we have been trying to reach you about your body's extended warranty

welcome to my twisted ankles, which tear tendons from my heels and stretch my calves lute-string tight, flexed feet scraping cracked skin against silk sheets in vain efforts to mitigate my muscle tension. i'd suspect i was born to be the boneless girl i dragged through adobe flash bubbles in fifth grade study hall were it not for the fact that sometimes cracking my neck makes me sick in a way that butter or cream never could. i could walk on rose petals for eternity to sate high-maintenance hammertoes and my wrists would both still beg *snap me before the swelling bursts open, bitch. don't you feel the shifts in your crooked bones, your jaw piercing your chin as your teeth abscess?* i've so exceeded expectations of normal wear and tear that i can't help but aspire to splinter as a spruce would, pinprick gnarls in the heels of enemies.

in which i perforate

i.   something about gender euphoria
and a newfound love for fashion at age
eleven looked like thousands of screenshots
of virtual paper dolls pasted into microsoft
paint landscapes. my kind of little girl dragged
boyclothes over girldolls, sometimes finding
fits but also finding that bodies are only so fluid,
even onscreen where i can pretend i'm the taco bell
guzzling mallgoth of my dreams for a weekend.

ii.   there wasn't a pair of brindle uggs or a polo
shirt embroidered with a moose or seagull
that could make me girl enough for the schoolyard.
every shade of black and skulls i bought
on clearance said *fuck you, preps* a little more;
by summer vacation i'd sealed it with a trim
of permafrizzed dishwater hair from the small of my
back to the fold of ear cartilage i'd pierce
on a whim at twenty-two.

iii.   paradise was painted in lilly pulitzer palms
when i was five and my best friend's mom said
i was a winter, whatever that meant in the early
aughts, or before or after. i should have wanted
popstar eyelashes and french-tipped fingernails,
teengirl aquapink everything. when there was
no version of lady that fit her, my kind of little
girl settled for sculpting her dreamsuit on stardoll,
then bought it a boy-bodied basketball jersey to wear
with a pleated skirt and kitten heels in its bedroom.

voidspeak (shattered)

shattered asks: are there some things you can run out of chances to fix?

the void says: i know you are always mad at entropy—its way of slowly snapping your plans in half like a cheap plastic ruler, its chaos you could never plan for. i know it has splintered your tendons to nothingness in spots and made you sick at the mere thought of sweet cream in your stomach. i know you look at your body and see an unwieldy temple that should have been abandoned years ago, and some days you may even be right.

do you remember when you were in the sixth grade and really, actually liked a boy? you went to a dance you thought he'd be at and he never showed up. your orchidpink motorola razr quit you that night too, and even though the tiny screen declared its internal errors fatal, you still keep it in the drawer under the microwave. somehow it became a sentimental relic. so, while a repair may be out of the question, didn't you save that cell phone because there was still a hope within you that it could be possible at all?

save changes to untitled?

sometimes you pack a candle away and it reminds you > of how being alive again after being dead for so long is such a mindfuck > (last summer it took you as long to restart as a spent cell phone in august heat) > sometimes you > imagine money > imagine fame > imagine believing in God > imagine wearing a Don't Tread On Me shirt in 2022 > imagine not being addled by iced coffee > imagine the fever dream of reality > balloons tied up outside the city jail > *mez-amaro*[4] in a fancy bottle you're afraid to pour from > uneven ground, crooked horizon lines > fireworks so far away you can only see them > imagine remembering winter > its snowspeckled rooftops and smothered backyards as tall as my springer spaniel > sometimes anxiety fucks your imagination and then > sometimes all you can say to yourself is *cut it the fuck out*

---

[4] home-style amaro made with mezcal as a base spirit

free & for sale (yard sard)

this friday afternoon i will be under
a sycamore in the park outside
of my apartment with a variety of things
i've convinced myself to part with, including:

jingle bell stick, flamingo painting,
flat half-consumed ginger beer,
a Razzy Bailey record, half the candles
on my coffee table, everything that came
with Kinder eggs, two mini cacti, expired
canned beets, a drawing of a sinister
blob i never gave my ex, and maybe
an overshare if you talk to me nice enough.

consequences

do you know what a "big picture" is? what was it someone said once about how when you find that your lust for death has seeped as far as your marrow, you're reckless because there's no part of the future that registers in the burrow of grey matter where your brain once lived? did you know that one time i was on a date with another photographer who saw my work and said i should try zooming out and letting the details shrink away? did you know that the year before, someone else said i should focus on one photograph that spoke without any need for my words? why didn't that hurt more? do you think it's because co-star told me to imitate my reflection and that morning my bedhead looked like sex hair? do you think there's a chance i'm still too nearsighted to lose my recklessness? is that why i no longer wince at the weekly worming thoughts of long fingernails wiggling like loose teeth in my nail beds' cavities? why i can't seem to figure out how old i am or what my position is in the line to the grave?

self-assessment essay rejects

~~i want to go to grad school because i kind of fucking hate my life and i'm naively hoping this will help me hate it less.~~

~~i believe the opportunity to reimmerse myself in a community that validates me and my shitty choices might help the crushing wave of self doubt i am feeling.~~

~~as an artist, i am just trying to make work by literally any means possible so that i can continue to use my practice as an escape from reality under the guise of documenting that reality objectively.~~

~~it is my opinion that no one ever fucking listens to what i have to say anymore and therefore you now have to listen to me ramble on about influencers for half a paragraph.~~

~~i wish i could type this essay the way i type on discord and when i am texting my friends. i kind of feel like it'd prompt me to be more honest, but then again, that might be a bad thing.~~

oh my god if i make this fucking book part of my graduate thesis, people may actually read it, and i don't know if that's empowering or terrifying.

when i think of the quiet horror that is existing inside of my brain and body at this moment in time, i am overcome by a strenuous desire to delete everything i have ever posted on the internet ever and live in a yurt in my parents' backyard.

i relate very strongly to the song "hot mess" by late 2000s pop punk band cobra starship in that i would absolutely tattoo "i hate this place" inside my lip for art.

a thicket of weeds

there is no having seen it all as i'd once supposed > there are still pinpricks of shock drifting over me sometimes when i find love in something > when i look down at the page > at how my carpal tunnel syndrome told me not to write by hand for fear of shooting wrist pains up swollen knuckles > at the places i wander when i look for the second and third and fourth ways to polish a shoe > there are still pangs of delight deep in my guts > nearly stronger than any love i've felt in flesh > each time i feel my weight drop onto page or disappear through a lens into silver > each time i remember that evolution is a series of adaptive reactions > levels-up > and i am proving myself to be no exception > each time i ask if there is really something after all to the cliché of blooming where you are planted > because i've always loved the way that despite being laid bare at least twice a year > a thicket of weeds still found its way to the garden box outside my old house > to the fractures in asphalt highways through ghost towns > i've always loved that we call errant flowers volunteers with some sort of dignity > but mostly that through every attempt made to tear burdock and crabgrass up by roots > through all efforts towards aesthetic order > there are still seeds in the soil > in the air > that will scatter and flail > settle and root > and thrive wherever they land

the duality of void

in sunlight i adore you and tell you
twenty-seven times at least. i can't process
your fantasy face when you are upside-down,
looking up from bosom cushions, but i can still
see the citrine coronas of your irises in my
deepest-buried sunlit daydreams come alive.

> (on the latter, i still am in love, but my past tells
> me more awe is superfluous and dangerous—
> it's never served me well before.)

> and in lamplight i mount you with a pro wrestler's
> swagger, in leather and in glitter, with sweaty
> mangled mane and all. our valley of the end lies far
> beyond san fernando, my love—i am taking you
> to every airport and seaboard town you've ever
> so much as sighed at, and then back again.

> (on the former, i still want to flip over onto you
> like in my most depraved daydreams—
> i just don't see why we should limit ourselves.)

scorpius

tonight when i see
scorpius in the july
twilight i tug myself five

years backwards
to tie-dyed damask
across plaster

walls and scattered
over the ceiling like
cirrostratus ribbons.

rave lights knife
me like a half-dozen
shucked oysters.

hot sugar crush

i bought tigerbeat at the airport like everyone
else in my class but i used to look through
and strike through boys' faces with sharpie,

decreeing them and their fans disgusting
while hanging hilary duff posters on wildflower
pink walls. and it wasn't that boys

weren't for me, but that i had to be swayed
by coalblack tresses whose long waves would meld
so delicately with my freckles and beachglass

blue eyes, whose overdyed skinny jeans looked
just as good on spindly preteen legs as theirs,
whose love was as unattainable as their likeness.

i heart my fat ass

i want to know how i will write about the first night i actually felt queer.

i want to know how much of it i'll remember the way it is. the way i finally feel at home in my bedroom. the way i am wearing mens' underwear for the first day of my life. the way my jesus bong is just dumb enough to round out the whole aesthetic. the way the biggest tattoo i've ever gotten is absolutely throbbing on my leg right now. the way the candle makes this whole room smell exactly like hotel soaps from my childhood.

the 'babygirl' necklace that came with another one i wanted (and i said i'd only wear that one as a joke). the pink velvet duvet and the 70s thrift store watercolor sheets. the point and shoot on the tripod blocking the tv. the wedding planner no one knew i bought laying in the trash can. the sweating pickle jar of water on my nightstand. the discord pings and dreamland playing in the background. my housemate's shrug lighter. the brand new hitachi the size of my forearm in the bottom drawer. the confidence i never knew i had. the femininity i've been beaten into. everyone else's expectations.

waking up in the morning and realizing that clichés can still hold weight sometimes and that maybe this is actually the first day of the rest of my life. fluidity. freedom. sometimes anxiety, sometimes comfort. peace.

self portrait as a food blogger

recipe: butter and toast and jam

serves: two, if your appetite is
anything like mine.

i woke up picking at mosquito bites
on my calves, left by pests undeterred
by citronella or tobacco smoke because
i am the standing water
in which they breed.

i haven't been to the park since i've been
back, instead raising blinds and peeking
through walnut tree limbs, nearly immune
to sirens and church bells that kept me
up all night last time i lived here.

i am the shoeshine on daguerre's
paris street, surrounded by light trails
of houseflies circling a sweaty cerveza like
they would stray tuxedo cats dead on the highway,
housemates coming and going,
the sun's path over the roof to meet me back
in my bed each evening through
westward-facing windows.

the passage of time is measured
in the disappearing wax of fresh linen
candles on charcoal-stained countertops
and punctuated by the growling
of my stomach.

ingredients: a copious amount of the communal stick of butter sitting on the counter, two slices of store-brand italian bread, blueberry preserves in a whimsical glass jar that costs way too much money but looks nice in photos

preparation: place one piece of bread in each of the toaster's slats. set desired temperature and depress lever. stare out the window over the back fence for so long you forget you have something in the toaster. shriek and feel anxious for 5-8 minutes when it pops up. spread butter and blueberry preserves liberally over the toast with a small cheese knife.

author's note: be sure to enjoy promptly and avoid staring into space for long periods of time while eating, perhaps wondering if the preservation of the warm body that's standing in this phantom of a kitchen right now is really all you've accomplished since you moved out five years ago.

acknowledgements

Versions of pieces in this collection have previously appeared or are forthcoming in other publications, as follows:

- "i hate so much about the things that you choose to be" and "save changes to untitled?" (as "anxiety fucked my imagination") previously appeared in *Like a Girl Zine, Issue 5.*

- "in which dread pools and begins to percolate" previously appeared in the *cool rock repository kettle expo.*

- "self portrait as a food blogger" previously appeared in *Color Tag Magazine*'s *HIRAETH* zine, and was republished by *en*gendered lit.*

- "a thicket of weeds" previously appeared in *Gastropoda.*

- "episodic memory" previously appeared in *en*gendered lit.*

- "voidspeak (skinned)" and "we have been trying to reach you about your body's extended warranty" previously appeared in *black stone / white stone review*'s *Making the Machines that Destroy Us* zine. (July 2022)

- "in which i kind of want to live in schitt's creek" previously appeared in *Dollar Store Magazine, Issue 4: Pop Culture, But Make It Pedantic.* (July 2022)

- "failed self portrait as link from *the legend of zelda: breath of the wild*" previously appeared in *Sage Cigarettes.* (August 2022)

- "scorpius" previously appeared in *celestite poetry, Issue 5.* (September 2022)

- "hot sugar crush" previously appeared in *eggplant tears, issue 1: soft-boiled.* (September 2022)

- "who has a gps map of hell i can borrow?" and "searching" previously appeared in *the winnow magazine*'s *Digital Wastelands* issue. (October 2022)

- "assigned cybernetic at birth" and "we have been trying to reach you about your body's extended warranty" previously appeared in *Spoonie Magazine.* (October 2022)

- "in which i perforate" previously appeared in *Spilled Ink* by *Hooligan Magazine.* (October 2022)

- "you may find yourself" and "rot around the edges" previously appeared in *the winnow magazine*'s *Home/Liminal Spaces* issue. (November 2022)

- "clamshell" previously appeared in *Good Luck Have Fun Press, Issue 1.* (December 2022)

- "the duality of void" previously appeared in *Delicate Friend, Issue 9.* (December 2022)

- "chicken" previously appeared in Powders Press, *Issue 4: Spectrum.* (January 2023)

- "free & for sale (iso wholeness)," "free & for sale (selling shame)," and "free & for sale (yard sard)" previously appeared in *Bullshit Lit.* (January 2023)

- "eroding" previously appeared in Querencia Press' *Winter 2023 Anthology.* (January 2023)

- "a haibun of indifference to my body" previously appeared in *The Bitchin' Kitsch, Volume 14 Issue 1.* (January 2023)

- "personal evolution as alchemy" previously appeared in *the lickety-split*. (February 2023)

- "in which i write myself backwards" is forthcoming in *The Elpis Letters*. (May 2023)

thanks

Mom, Dad, Andrew, Mads, Kendall, Sean, Lohr, Jamie, Scills, Sarah, Robin, Kayla, Bree, Natalie, Tommy, Emily

CPSIA information can be obtained
at www.ICGtesting.com
Printed in the USA
BVHW052103100323
660193BV00006B/63